because two are better than one

you
and
me
Mom

HOWARD
PUBLISHING CO.

Printed in Mexico

Linda M. Wall

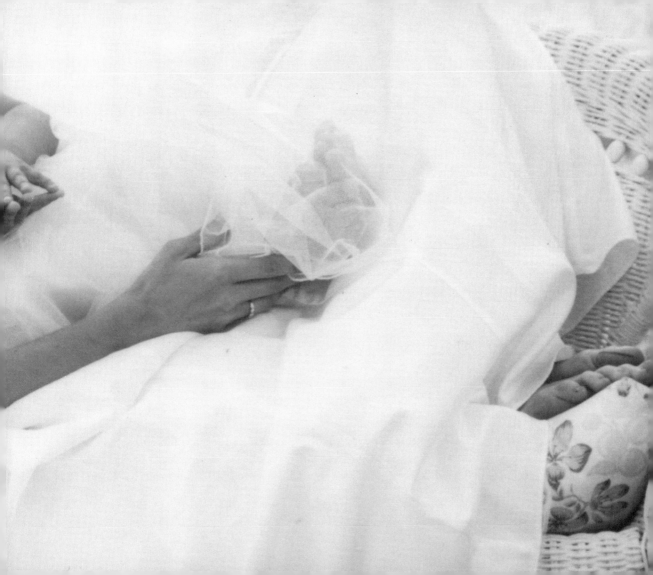

*You've always been my anchor,
holding me to what's true.*

Mom

A mother is she
who can take the place
of all others but whose place
no one else can take.

Cardinal Mermillod

Constance Fielding's Daughter

"Excuse me, nurse."

Amanda Blackstone stepped in front of a frazzled healthcare worker, halting the woman's determined progress down the hospital corridor. "I'm looking for my mother, Constance Fielding. I understand she's on this floor."

The nurse gave Amanda a visual once-over and consulted the clipboard in her hand.

"Hmmm, let me see here." She dragged a finger down a list of patient names. "Fielding, Fielding . . ."

Amanda shifted her leather briefcase from one hand to the other, her high-heeled shoe tapping an impatient rhythm on the vinyl floor.

"Room 2214, down the hall."

Amanda thanked her and continued along the hushed hallway, cringing at the explosive sound of her heels. No wonder nurses wore soft-soled shoes—this place was a virtual echo chamber. She held her breath, a defensive maneuver against the odors that assaulted her nose.

Here, 2214—finally. Amanda tiptoed into the room, bracing herself for the unknown. Her father's message had said only that her mother was hurt and in the hospital.

"Mom?"

"Amanda!"

Her mother sat propped up in bed, a sheepish grin on her face. Her right ankle was wrapped, and her forehead sported a small bandage. Amanda's father lounged in the chair beside the bed, a magazine open on his lap.

Amanda took stock of her mother's injuries and, after reassuring herself that they were minor, relaxed her stance. She lowered her briefcase to the floor and planted a hand on one hip.

"All right, Mother. What was it this time? Rock climbing? In-line skating? Bungee jumping?" Her relief inched toward irritation with each query she shot off.

Her mother batted the air with her hand. "A little mishap with an all-terrain vehicle. No big deal. I have a concussion, so they want to keep me overnight. But I'll be up to my old tricks in no time."

That's what I'm afraid of.

For a split second, Amanda wished her mother's injuries were greater. Maybe then she'd think twice about taking these ridiculous risks. Her head began to throb. She pressed her fingertips to her temples.

"Mother, you make me crazy! Sixty-five years old, and you act like some hormone-driven teenager." She paced the small hospital room. "An all-terrain vehicle—for heaven's sake! Why can't you stay home and bake cookies or knit, like other women your age?"

Her mother laughed. "Because my cookies burn, and I don't know how to knit. Personally, I think those needles look dangerous. Besides, I like adventure."

Amanda blew out an exasperated breath and glared at the ceiling. *This is going nowhere.* She turned to her father.

"Daddy, you talk to her."

Her father shrugged, amusement lighting his eyes. "Sorry, kiddo. Your mother's always been her own person. I can't change that." He gave his wife an affectionate pat on the arm. "God broke the mold on this old girl."

Her mother and father exchanged conspiratorial grins. Amanda moaned. She was fighting a losing battle while her father aided and abetted the enemy. *Traitor.*

She shook her head, jaw tensed. She needed to leave before she said something she'd regret. She made a show of studying her watch.

"Look, I have to get home." She leveled a manicured finger at her mother. "But we're not through talking about this, Mom. Daddy might think this second childhood of yours is cute, but frankly, I don't need the aggravation."

Amanda ignored the warning bells going off in her head and pressed on. "What I need is for you to grow up, Mother!"

She pretended she didn't see her mother draw back as if she'd been slapped, tears filling her eyes. Amanda snatched her briefcase and left the room.

"Grandma rode an ATV? Cool!" Twelve-year-old Lacey stretched across the table, helping herself to another roll and knocking over the salt shaker with her arm.

Amanda swatted her daughter's hand. "How many times do I have to tell you? Ask. Don't reach.

"And your grandmother's exploits are not 'cool'—they're dangerous. Stubborn woman! I told her to stop taking chances. She just smiled and said, 'I like adventure.'"

Amanda's husband, Tom, chuckled. "Sounds like Constance. She's really something."

Amanda rolled her eyes. "She's something, all right." She sipped her coffee, casting about for a more comfortable topic of conversation. "So, Lacey, how was your day?"

Lacey finished her milk and wiped her mouth with the back of her hand. Amanda grimaced.

"OK, I guess. Except Sasha and Emily keep bugging me to try out for the dance team. I don't really want to. I'd rather play soccer."

Amanda picked up a roll and her butter knife, relieved to be back on safe conversational ground. "So, then, play soccer if that's what you want."

"Yeah, but my friends want me to do dance."

Amanda stopped buttering her roll and shook her knife at Lacey. "Look, baby, you do what *you* want. Don't let other people make you into someone you're not. You be the person you want to be, and don't worry about what others think."

Amanda glanced at Tom for support. He cocked one eyebrow, a grin tugging at the corners of his mouth.

She narrowed her eyes at him. "What?"

Tom blinked, the picture of innocence. "Nothing."

"All I said was that Lacey shouldn't let other people pressure her to be someone she's not—"

Tom pushed away from the table, his chair legs scraping the floor. A hint of a smile still played at his lips. "My turn to do dishes."

Amanda frowned. "Wait just a minute! You think that's what I'm doing to Mom, don't you? You think because I want her to be safe, I'm trying to make her into someone she's not?"

Tom and an armload of dirty dishes disappeared without comment into the kitchen. Amanda shouted at his retreating backside.

"That is *not* what I'm doing! I'm trying to watch out for her."

When he didn't answer, she looked at Lacey. "Right?"

Lacey, employing her usual adolescent diplomacy, responded with a shrug and attacked her dessert.

Of course I'm right, Amanda fumed. She drummed her fingernails on the table, wondering why right suddenly felt so inexplicably wrong.

Amanda arrived at the hospital the next morning amid the din of breakfast carts clattering through the halls. She hesitated outside her mother's room and shifted the package under her arm.

Here goes. She shoved open the door and collided with a spinning wheelchair.

"Mother, what on earth—?"

Her mother blushed and backed the chair away from the door.

"Sorry. I just wanted to see if this thing would do a wheelie." She fumbled with the brakes. "Hospital rules, you know. Heaven forbid they'd let anyone *walk* out of here on their own steam."

Amanda smoothed the skirt of her gray business suit, regaining her composure. "So, does it?"

"What?"

"The wheelchair. Does it do wheelies?"

Her mother responded with a rueful smile. "Not really."

They fell silent. Amanda noticed the packed overnight bag on the bed.

"Dad's picking you up?"

"Yes."

The exchange was stiff and uncomfortable, like an overstarched shirt. Amanda's harsh words from the day before seemed to dangle in the air between them. *Grow up, Mother!*

"Mom, what I said yesterday—"

Her mother held up a hand. "Let's just leave it, Amanda. I know you don't approve of my activities. But I can't change—even for you."

"I know, Mom." Amanda had to laugh. "Up until last night I thought you *had* changed! Now I realize I'm the one who's become someone different."

Her mother looked confused. Amanda knelt beside her wheelchair and opened the package she'd brought, revealing a worn photo album.

"Remember this? I found it last night."

Her mother brightened. "Oh, my. I haven't seen that in decades."

Amanda opened the book and flipped the pages. "Mother-daughter horse camp, remember? Look at this. Pictures of you—and me—doing risky things like barrel racing and jumping!" She shook her head. "Whatever happened to that adventurous little girl, anyway?"

Her mother patted her hand. "I guess she grew up."

"Maybe. Or maybe, somewhere along the way, she forgot who she was—Constance Fielding's daughter."

Amanda blinked back a tear and turned the wheelchair so she could face her mother.

"Mom, I don't want you to change. When I finally grow up, I hope I'm just like you."

"I doubt the world is ready for that."

"Well, then, are you ready for this?" With a flourish, Amanda produced a glossy brochure. "A deluxe mountain trail ride on horseback—for two!"

"Two? You mean, you and me?"

Amanda grinned. "Well, somebody has to watch out for you. Just promise me this place has a sleepy old nag with my name on her—and no jumping!"

"Oh, come on. Just once?"

"Mother—"

Her mother held up her hands in surrender. "OK, OK. We'll start slowly." She looked at Amanda, her eyes moist. "Friends?"

"Friends. Now about that knitting . . . "

Ten Lessons I Learned from My Mother

1 It's never too late to try something new.

2 Don't be afraid to say what you think—just make sure you think before you say it.

3 Be genuine, rather than merely copying others around you.

4 No matter how old you get, you're always your mother's baby.

5 A bad day can often be improved with a little humor and a healthy dose of chocolate.

6

A gentle response accomplishes
more than a harsh retort.

7

When you fall down,
get up and try again.

8

Share what
you have with
someone who
doesn't.

9

Make plans for
your life, but don't be
surprised if God has
a different idea.

10

No family phone call or
visit is complete without an
"I love you."

thank

you...

*for encouraging me
to be myself.*

A TRIBUTE TO MOM

Golden Opportunity

My mother planned to fill her retirement days with ceramics classes, gardening, and grandchildren. I was behind that 100 percent. She had worked hard all her life— she deserved to kick back and relax. But when the golden opportunity finally came, we were both in for a surprise.

Mom broke the news to me as gently as she could. God was calling her and my stepfather to pack up and travel halfway around the globe to minister on another continent—for an undetermined period of time. No ceramics, no gardening, no visits to daughter and grandkids.

No way, I thought. *You belong at home, not on the other side of the ocean!* This wasn't what I wanted at all, but I knew better than to argue with God (aloud any-way). I bit my tongue and tried to be happy.

When the day came, Mom and I hugged each other and exchanged tearful good-byes. Then she flew away, leaving her family behind. I prayed she'd get it out of her system and hurry home.

It was more than two years before she returned. I needed only one look at that radiant face to know I'd have been wrong to try to keep Mom home those two years. God had used her in amazing ways because she had set aside her plans and the expec-tations of others to follow Him.

I was more proud of her in that moment than I had ever been.

God has made everything beautiful

for its own time. . . . So I concluded

that there is nothing better for

people than to be happy and to enjoy

themselves as long as they can.

And people should eat and drink

and enjoy the fruits of their labor,

for these are gifts from God.

—Ecclesiastes 3:11–13 NLT

Dear one-of-a-kind Mom,

You are a priceless work of art. You've always been who you are, exactly who God made you to be, beautiful, the best. You have shown me that there's no age limit on happiness and fun, and that everything we do, everything we have, and the people we become are priceless gifts from God.

Your admiring child

*You delayed your dreams
so I could follow mine.*

Mom

As a mother, my job
is to take care of what is possible
and trust God
with the impossible.

Ruth Bell Graham

First Day of School

Shelby Hammond flung open the door of her apartment, ready to pounce on whoever dared ring her doorbell at 6:30 in the morning.

Not that she had been sleeping—anxiety over the day ahead had eliminated any chance of that hours ago. Still, the last thing she needed today, of all days, was an early morning interruption.

She peered at the woman standing on her front porch, the familiar lavender warmup suit and petite stature quickly identified her visitor.

"Mom, what in the world are you doing here?"

Shelby's mother raised two steaming cups in salute.

"Mocha with mint, two shots, lots of whipped cream. Just the way you like it." She shrugged a shoulder. "I thought maybe you could use a boost this morning."

Shelby forgot her irritation and eagerly reached for one of the drinks. She brought the cup to her face, closed her eyes, and breathed in the soothing aroma. With a satisfied grin, she waved her mother into the apartment and shut the door.

Mother and daughter carried their coffee across the room and settled beside each other on the couch. Shelby took a long drink, savoring the rich blend of chocolate and mint.

"Mmmm. You know me well, Mom." A gentle sigh escaped her lips. "Too bad I can't stuff you in my pocket and take you with me today."

Her mother laughed. "First day of school jitters, huh?" She gave Shelby's knee a reassuring squeeze. "You'll do just fine, honey. You're going to be a fantastic teacher."

"I hope so." Shelby wrapped her hands around her coffee, the hot liquid warming her skin through the paper container.

"To tell you the truth, Mom, I feel more like one of my new little kindergarten students than their teacher. I'm as nervous now as I was on *my* first day of kindergarten!"

Her mother smiled, her face alive with the memory. "You were scared to death. It was all I could do to convince you to stay there until I came back."

"Loaning me that old plastic key chain of yours did the trick," Shelby said. "Remember? The one with the picture frame that held that goofy photo of the two of us we took at the mall. You let me keep it on the first day of school."

Her mother nodded. "I thought it might help you remember you were loved and that I'd be waiting for you at the end of the day."

"Well, it worked. I kept it in my pocket, and every time I got scared, I looked at it. I didn't feel so lonely when I saw your face."

Shelby and her mom sipped their coffee in companionable silence.

"Wonder whatever happened to that old key chain, anyway," Shelby said after a few minutes. Then, with a glance at her watch, she sprang up from the couch.

"Wow, look at the time! Mom, this has been great, but I've got to get ready, or I'll be late."

Her mother stood and waved her off with a hand. "You go ahead, dear. How about if I make your lunch while you get dressed?"

Shelby shot her mother a grateful look. She could always count on Mom to know just what she needed.

"That'd be terrific, Mom. Thanks." She threw her arms around her mother and pulled her close in a bear hug. "And thanks for bringing the coffee. It was perfect."

She hurried to her bedroom, leaving her mother to putter in the kitchen.

Forty-five minutes later, dressed in a crisp summer blouse and khaki skirt, Shelby stood for a final inspection.

"How do I look?"

Her mother nodded her approval. "Like a teacher. A beautiful, talented, first-rate teacher."

Shelby laughed. "Well, I'm glad you're not biased or anything." She grabbed her book bag from the chair by the door, stuffing inside it the lunch her mother had made.

The two women left the apartment together, arms linked as they walked to the parking lot.

"Call me tonight," Shelby's mother said at the door of her car.

"I will. Pray for me today, will you?"

"I always do."

"Good morning, boys and girls. I'm your teacher, Miss Hammond." Shelby beamed at the cherubic faces looking back at her with wide-eyed anticipation.

Bolstered by caffeine and her mother's reassurance, she felt invincible. She could handle anything—even little Trevor, who seemed determined to break all the rules in his first hour of school.

After pulling Trevor down from the window ledge for the second time that morning, Shelby directed the children to sit cross-legged around her on the "reading rug." Holding Trevor captive beside her, she repeated the classroom rules.

" . . . keep your hands and feet to yourselves, follow directions, and raise your hand to talk. Does anyone have a question?"

A girl with braids thrust her arm in the air and waved it furiously.

"Yes, Missy, thank you for raising your hand. What's your question?"

"Are you married?"

Shelby smiled. "No, not yet."

Trevor wriggled in her grasp, trying to reach another student with his foot. Shelby tightened her hold and looked around at the rest of the students.

"Are there any questions about school?"

Another hand went up, a little boy this time.

"Yes, Robert?"

"Well, then, do you got a dog?"

Trevor momentarily ceased his struggles to break free, apparently interested in this topic. Shelby relaxed her arm around him and shook her head.

"No. No dogs, no cats, no pets at all."

Seeing an opportunity, Trevor ducked under her arm and ran for the door. Shelby caught him before he escaped into the hallway. *That would be all I'd need—to lose a student on my first day!*

She brought him, kicking and screaming, back to the group and held him in front of her in a two-armed hug.

After a half dozen more inquiries into her social life and what she had eaten for breakfast, Shelby decided to abandon question time and move on to art.

Trevor lit up at the prospect of glue and glitter, solemnly promising to behave. Shelby released him to join his classmates at the tables while she explained the project.

"Boys and girls, today we're going to—"

A hand shot up. Shelby suppressed a frustrated sigh. So far it seemed teaching was more about managing interruptions than imparting knowledge.

"Jennifer, do you have something to say about our art project?"

Jennifer shook her head. "No, Teacher."

"Well, we're talking about art now. OK?"

"OK. I just thought you should know Trevor is smearing glue on all the chairs."

The morning went downhill from there, taking Shelby's patience and confidence with it.

Trevor eventually earned a free trip to the principal's office. But even without her number one troublemaker, Shelby was beginning to feel like a chew toy in a pack of greedy puppies.

All twenty-two children demanded a piece of her as the morning wore on. They pulled on her arms, climbed onto her lap, whispered secrets in her ear, and cried on her shoulder until she felt like weeping too.

One little boy followed her all morning, his hand clutching the hem of her skirt.

"I want my mommy," he wailed.

That makes two of us.

Shelby nearly cheered out loud when snack time finally arrived. She passed around the apple juice and animal crackers, reveling in the quiet that followed. Her stomach growled as she watched the children devour their snacks. She rummaged in her lunch for a piece of fruit.

What in the world . . . ?

Shelby's hand touched something hard at the bottom of the bag. She frowned and pulled the mysterious object into the light.

She stared at it for a moment, her breath caught in her throat. Unexpected tears sprang to her eyes, blurring the pair of faces that grinned up at her.

"Mom," she whispered.

Shelby cradled the old plastic key chain in her hand, long-ago memories washing over her like a gentle rain. For an instant, she forgot everything else—her fatigue, her frustration, even Trevor.

One of the children finally broke the silence.

"What's the matter, Teacher?"

"She's crying," another child exclaimed, wonder in his voice.

"Are you OK, Teacher?"

The children left their snacks and crowded about her, round faces upturned and brows furrowed. Sticky hands patted her.

Shelby wiped her eyes and smiled at the five-year-olds huddled around her, offering what measure of comfort they could.

In that moment, she knew she'd make it. Her mom loved her and was praying for her. The old key chain was simply a reminder.

With another look at her mother's face in the picture, Shelby tucked the key chain in the pocket of her skirt and gave it a pat. Then she pulled the children into a group hug.

"Yes, I'm OK. More than OK. Now let's hurry and clean up. Before you know it, your mommies will be here for you."

Ten Things I Love to Do with My Mother

1 Catching up over a hot mocha or latte

2 Getting up before dawn and shopping the after-Thanksgiving, early-bird sales

3 Trading books and talking about our favorite scenes

4 Sharing a big holiday meal with all the trimmings

5 Going for a brisk walk (especially after that big holiday meal)

6 Collecting shells and agates on the beach

7 Laughing at ourselves in old photographs

8 Playing marathon board games

9 Browsing through bookstores, even though neither of us needs any more books

10 Going to church

thank

you...

for believing in me and never giving up even when I wanted to give up on myself.

Being There

Mothers have a way of being there for their kids, even when life separates them physically. Whether across town or across an ocean, it seems like moms intuitively know how to be present in spirit, if not in body.

When I gave birth to my first daughter, I felt a jumble of emotions—elation, excitement, pride. And fear. I was a competent, educated professional, but when it came to caring for a new little life, I felt terrified. I needed my mom.

And she came. The day my husband and I brought our bundle of joy home from the hospital, Mom was there to offer wisdom and a helping hand. After a few days, however, she had to go home, and I was on my own.

But Mom left me something. It was a small, faded ceramic planter, shaped like an open book with gilt-edged pages. The pages bore the word *Congratulations*, accompanied by a delicate painting of an infant.

I remembered that old planter from my childhood. Someone—perhaps my grandma—had given it to my mother on the birth of her first child. And now Mom was handing it down to me, a reminder that she had been a new mom once too. Without speaking a word, Mom let me know I was not alone.

That's my mom. She has always been there for me, one way or another, quietly encouraging and rooting me on.

My mother—my friend.

Though the mountains be shaken

and the hills be removed, yet my

unfailing love for you will not be

shaken.

—Isaiah 54:10

Dear Mom,

One thing I've always been able to count on is your love. Knowing that, even when my world was crumbling around me, you'd be there with an encouraging word and a warm hug has given me courage. And it has taught me how to love. So, no matter what life brings us in the future, know that I love you. And I always will.

Your loving child

Mom

Walks along a sandy beach
and coffee breaks for two;
late-night talks, heart to heart,
between us, me and you.

When I was young, I never guessed
the blessing it would be
to one day find that you, my mom,
are now a friend to me.

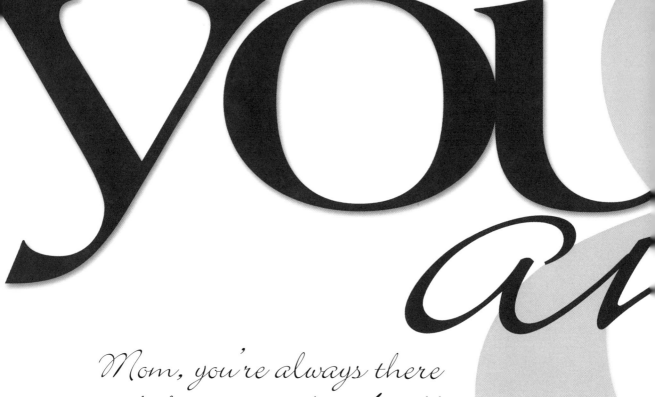

Mom, you're always there
to help me up when I fall
and to lead me back home
when I've lost my way.

Mom

Motherhood is being available
to your children
whenever they need you,
no matter what their age or need.

Doris Pengilly

Better Together

"Mom, this church campout is soooo lame! I don't see why I have to waste my weekend with a bunch of people I don't even know." Morgan Donnelly flopped onto a lawn chair outside their two-person tent, arms crossed and temper smoldering.

Her mother, who was digging through the camping equipment in the trunk of their car, gave no discernible response. Morgan scowled and kicked up a cloud of dust with her toe.

"This weekend is going to be such a drag."

"Aha!" Her mother jerked upright and held aloft a metal coffeepot like an Academy Award. "We're in business now!"

Morgan rolled her eyes skyward. "Mom, you aren't even listening!"

"Sure I am." Her mother slammed the trunk lid and carried her treasure to the water spigot. She filled it with water, spooned coffee into the basket, and settled the pot on the camp stove. Finally, she turned to Morgan.

"Look, sweetie, I know you don't want to be here. But this campout is a good way to get to know people in our new church. You'll make friends, you'll see."

"Mom, it's hot and it's dirty here"—Morgan swatted at a winged insect hovering near her arm—"and there are . . . like, a gazillion bugs! All my friends back where we used to live are probably spending their weekend someplace clean and bug free, like the mall!

"Besides, most of the kids here have been together forever. How am I supposed to break into their little clique? They aren't going to want me crowding in."

Her mother drew up a chair beside her. "Not true, honey. These kids will love you. Just give them a chance." She sat down and began to look over the printed schedule of events for the weekend.

"Hey, here's an idea." Morgan's mom flicked the paper with her fingernail. "There's going to be a talent show tomorrow night. You could sing."

Morgan bolted from her chair as if she'd been stung. "No way, Mom! I'm not singing in front of all these strangers. Forget it. Nope. *Not* happening."

"Come on, Morgan. Singing in the talent show would give the other kids a chance to see who you are. At our old church, people used to love to hear you and Dad . . . "

Morgan winced at the mention of her father—the man who had walked out on them six months ago without even looking back. Her mother's sentence trailed off, unfinished. Except for the hiss of the propane stove and the background clamor of adjoining campsites, it was oppressively quiet.

"Don't talk to me about Dad," Morgan said, spitting out each syllable. "I told you. I don't even want to hear his name."

"Morgan—" Her mother reached for her hand. Morgan backed away, shoving both hands deep into the pockets of her shorts.

"I'm going for a walk."

She strode to the wooded area behind their tent, ignoring her mother's pleas for her to wait. She randomly selected a narrow footpath from a maze of choices and embarked on it. The underbrush scratched at her legs as she moved deeper into the woods.

She wished she had worn something more protective than flip-flops and shorts.

Why did Mom have to go and bring up Dad? Morgan hated him for leaving. It was *his* fault Mom had to go back to work to make ends meet. It was *his* fault they had to move a hundred miles from their friends so Mom could find a decent job. And it was *his* fault Morgan was spending her weekend with total strangers!

The more Morgan thought about her dad, the angrier she became and the farther she wandered from camp. Whenever the trail forked off in different directions, she simply chose one and kept walking.

After about thirty minutes, Morgan stopped to catch her breath. She cocked her head and listened. She could no longer hear voices calling out or campfires crackling or dogs barking. Only the summer breeze rustling the leaves.

She looked behind her at the tangle of trails crisscrossing each other and felt a rush of panic. Which one led back to camp?

"OK, Morgan. Stay calm." She studied the paths, but each trail looked exactly like the next. "Oh, man," she muttered. "I've done it up good this time."

She picked a path, breathed a quick prayer, and started in what she hoped was the direction back to camp. After several minutes, however, she still didn't see anything familiar.

Maybe if she yelled, Mom would hear. Morgan never liked to admit when she needed help, but she was getting hungry—and being in the woods alone was starting to creep her out. She sucked in a breath and hollered at the top of her lungs.

"Mom! Hey, Mom!"

Nothing.

She tried again, louder this time. "M-o-mm!"

Still no response. Morgan chewed on her thumbnail and considered her predicament. If she wasn't so scared, the whole thing might actually be funny. What she wouldn't give to be back at that stupid campground with all those strangers now!

She found a fallen tree and, after inspecting for bugs, dropped down on it to rest. She hugged her knees to her chest and glanced around the sunlit woods, wondering what it might be like when the sun went down.

She shook her head. "Come on, Morgan. Have a little faith." She began to hum, then tested out a few timid words to a show tune she had learned in her school choir.

"Anything you can do, I can do better . . . "

Singing helped Morgan feel a little less lonely and afraid, so she stood up and sang the next line with gusto.

"I can do anything better than you!"

A murmur like a voice sounded in the distance. She stopped, her ears straining. *Probably just my own echo,* she thought.

She started singing again. "No you can't . . . "

She waited and heard a faint, but clear response. "Yes I can . . . "

She grinned, relief flooding her body. *Thank You, God!* She belted out the next line.

"No you can't!"

Then, still a distance away but closer now, came the reply. "Yes I cannnnnnn!"

"Mom! Mom!" Morgan ran in the direction of the voice. She stumbled through the underbrush, calling as she ran. "Mom, over here!"

"Morgan!" A familiar figure came into view. Morgan threw herself into her mother's arms.

"Mom, am I glad to see you!"

Her mother hugged her tight. "I heard you singing. Come on. Let's head back while I can still remember how I got here."

Morgan grabbed her mother's hand, stopping her. "Mom, I'm sorry I took off like that. It's just that talking about Dad makes me crazy sometimes. I hate what he did to us."

A sad smile crossed her mom's face. "I know. I hate it too. But we'll get through it." Her mother started down a path, then over her shoulder she added, "We're just going to have to trust God—and stick together."

Morgan fell in behind her. "Well, I'm with you there. If I've learned anything this afternoon, it's that together is better than alone when you're lost!"

They walked on in silence with her mother expertly negotiating the labyrinth of trails. Morgan was content to follow along behind, confident in her mom's ability to lead them out of the woods.

The buzz of activity from the campground grew louder. Morgan knew they were getting close. She could almost smell Mom's coffee. *Funny*, she thought. *It feels a little like coming home.* When they broke into the clearing behind their tent, Morgan draped an arm around her mom's shoulders.

"So . . . we don't have to tell anybody about my being lost in the woods, do we? I mean, I'm already the new kid on the block. I don't really think I need *that* black mark against me too."

Her mother laughed. "It'll be our secret."

"Oh, and one other thing . . . " Morgan hesitated. Her mother turned to look at her. Morgan swallowed hard and pressed on.

"Um . . . I thought I might just go ahead and, uh, see about—you know—singing in the talent show tomorrow night . . . maybe." There, she'd said it.

Her mother's face registered surprise. "Well, great."

"Yeah." Morgan flashed a mischievous grin. "I mean, how are these people going to know what a radically cool kid I am if I don't show them?"

Her mother smiled back. "So true, so true."

"But I do have one condition."

Her mother lifted her eyebrows and waited.

Morgan lowered her eyes and kicked at a broken twig on the ground. "I thought it might be nice if . . . if maybe you would sing with me. I mean, you have to admit we had a pretty good practice session back there."

Her mother looked like she had something in her eye. She sniffed and wiped at it. Then she said, "I would really like that, Morgan."

"Yeah, well, like you said, we have to stick together."

Ten Qualities
of a Terrific Mom

1 *She can keep a secret.*

2 *She bakes cookies or knows the best kind to buy.*

3 *She can fix any hurt.*

4 *She laughs at your jokes, no matter how many times she's heard them.*

5 *She listens, even if she's busy.*

6 She treats all problems seriously, no matter how silly they might seem to someone else.

7 She believes in you and never misses an opportunity to say, "You can do it."

8 She worries about you even when you're grown and have kids of your own.

9 She knows just the right way to make your favorite sandwich.

10 You can always talk to her, even in the middle of the night or during her favorite TV show.

thank

you...

for showing me the right path to walk
in life and for traveling it with me.

A TRIBUTE TO MOM

Leading the Way Home

When I was little, I occasionally toddled away from the safety of my mother's side—trailing after a novelty that caught my eye or following a skirt I thought was Mom's but which belonged to a stranger. When the novelty disappeared or the face above the skirt proved unfamiliar, I realized I was lost.

Finding my way back to where I belonged was uncomplicated in those early days. All I had to do was stop dead in my tracks and holler at the top of my pint-sized lungs, "Mo-mm-y!" and Mom would come to the rescue.

When I grew older, I didn't physically wander away, but poor choices sometimes landed me far from where I belonged. By that time, I was too proud and too independent to cry out for help. *I'm not lost,* I would tell myself. *I'm exploring!* And I stubbornly continued down paths that led me farther from home and safety.

Mom was always nearby in those moments, waiting for me to admit defeat and call for help. Kind of like God, I realize now. And when I finally swallowed my pride, Mom was there to help me find my way back home again.

So, thanks, Mom. Thank you for letting me struggle and wander, because that's how I learned. And most of all, thanks for finding me and leading me back where I belonged.

Two are better than one, because

they have a good return for their

work: If one falls down, his friend

can help him up. . . . Though one

may be overpowered, two can

defend themselves.

—Ecclesiastes 4:9–10, 12

My best friend, Mom,

　　When I was little, you were always right there to pick me up and make everything better when I fell. Somehow, no matter how old I am, you still do that. I don't know what I'd do without you, but I'm glad that as our relationship matures, we can be there for each other. Together, we're an invincible team!

Your grateful child

Your actions showed me how to behave. Your words taught me how to speak. Your heart taught me how to love.

Mom

Mothers play the leading roles
in giving birth to little souls.

Helen Steiner Rice

Presents from God

Jody Ann froze in place on the sidewalk, her brown lunch bag clutched to her chest. She could feel her heart thumping under her favorite pink sweater. With a sweaty palm, she pushed her heavy glasses back up her nose and squinted at the sign on the building in front of her. She already knew what it said, but she sounded out the words anyway.

"Lit-tle . . . Treas-ures . . . Child . . . " The next word was a tricky one. "De-vel-op-ment . . . Development . . . Cen-ter. Little Treasures Child Development Center."

Jody Ann's heart began to beat faster. *A real job!* She swallowed hard and tightened her hand around her lunch bag.

You can do it, Jody Ann. After all, she was twenty-two years old now—time to show Mama she could do something important. Her feet still wouldn't move.

A voice called from behind her. "Jody Ann, honey, are you sure you don't want me to walk in with you?"

Jody Ann closed her eyes. "Go home, Mama," she whispered. "Please, go home." She loved Mama more than anybody in the whole world, but she had to do this by herself.

She turned to see her mother leaning across the steering wheel of the family car, watching through the open window. Jody Ann put on her best smile.

"Don't worry, Mama. I'll do good."

Mama still didn't leave, so Jody Ann waved. "Bye, Mama. See you later. Bye!"

She waved until Mama's car slowly pulled away from the curb and disappeared down the street. Then, before she could change her mind, Jody Ann forced herself up the walk to the front door of the building.

She tugged open the heavy door and stepped inside. She stopped there, wiping first one sweaty hand and then the other on her pants. *Maybe Mama should have stayed.*

"May I help you?"

Jody Ann jumped at the voice. A lady behind a long counter was looking at her. She opened her mouth to answer her, but no words came. She ducked her head and twisted the top of her lunch bag between her fingers.

"Oh, you must be Jody Ann, our new volunteer," the lady said. She sounded nice. Jody Ann peered over the top of her smudged glasses.

"Y-yes," she stammered. "I am helping with th—the . . . babies."

"Wonderful! I'm Myra. Let me show you around."

Jody Ann followed Myra through room after room of little children. She had to take careful baby steps to make sure she didn't trip over the little ones playing on the floor. She tried hard to remember the names of the workers, but they got mixed up in her head.

I'm glad the babies have their names stuck on their clothes!

Myra took Jody Ann's lunch—to keep it safe, she said—and left her with a helper named Stephanie. "Just get to know the children for now, Jody Ann. I'm meeting with some students from the high-school newspaper, but I'll be back later."

Jody Ann watched Myra walk into the hall where two high-school girls giggled and smacked their gum. They stared at Jody Ann. She felt her face get hot and turned away.

She pushed up her glasses and looked around the room. Some of the children were taking naps. Others played with toys. Jody Ann thought she might like to play too, then she remembered. *I'm a helper now. But . . . how do I help?*

She spotted a girl sitting alone, rocking and banging a toy pot on the floor. She was bigger than the little babies, but she seemed more like them than the children her size.

"That's Rachel," Stephanie said. "She *loves* to rock and bang. Don't you, Rachel?"

The little girl didn't answer. She just kept rocking and banging. *Maybe she's special—like me*, Jody Ann thought.

She squatted down and smiled at the girl. "Rachel is a nice name. Mama told me a Bible story about Rachel."

Rachel didn't look up, but she smiled just a little when Jody Ann said her name. That felt good.

Jody Ann started to follow Stephanie to another part of the room, and Rachel made a loud screechy sound.

Stephanie laughed. "She wants you to stay, Jody Ann. I think she likes you." Another child began to cry. "I have to go. Don't worry, Rachel. Jody Ann will take care of you. She's a good helper."

Stephanie's words made Jody Ann feel proud. "I am a good helper," she said aloud. She sat down on the floor, and while her new friend banged her pot, Jody Ann told her about the "Bible Rachel." Rachel made a happy sound whenever Jody Ann said her name.

Some spit dribbled down Rachel's chin. "Uh-oh." Jody Ann looked around for something to wipe the girl's face. "Wait a minute."

She headed for a box of tissues across the room and was coming back with it when she saw the two high-school girls peeking in. Myra wasn't with them. Jody Ann stopped.

One of the girls pointed at Rachel. "What were her parents thinking, bringing a kid like that into the world?"

The other girl blew a pink bubble with her gum and popped it. "No kidding. Can you say *abortion*?"

The first girl laughed. Then she looked at Jody Ann. She bumped her friend with her elbow and said something about two retards. They giggled. Then one of them said, "Come on, let's go. We've got enough stuff for our article."

Jody Ann stared at the floor. She didn't know what a *'bortion* was, but she had heard the word *retard* lots of times.

She hunkered down by Rachel and wiped her chin. *How many times will Rachel get called a retard in her life? As many as me?* Thinking about that made Jody Ann want to cry. She patted Rachel's back and sang softly.

"Je-sus loves me, this I know . . . "

⌒

"Mama, what's a—a . . . 'bortion?" Jody Ann stood in the doorway of Mama's bedroom that night. She couldn't sleep.

Mama sat up and turned on a light. She rubbed her eyes, then patted the place beside her.

"Here, climb in. It's cold."

Jody Ann snuggled under the covers, then Mama said, "Abortion. That's a big word for so late at night. Where did you hear it?"

Jody Ann told Mama about Rachel and the girls from the high school. "What's a 'bortion, Mama?" she asked again.

Mama let out a long breath. "Well . . . it's a way to keep a baby from being born."

Jody Ann sat up and frowned. That didn't sound right. "Wh-why would a mama do that?"

"Well, sometimes the doctor says the baby will have problems if she's born, and maybe the parents think it might be . . . better not to have the baby."

The tears in Mama's eyes confused Jody Ann. She stuck out her lower lip and tried to understand. "Like . . . a special baby? Like me?"

Mama nodded.

"So . . . those girls . . . w-were saying special babies . . . sh-shouldn't be born?" Jody Ann thought for a minute. "But Rachel's mama didn't 'bortion her. And you . . . didn't 'bortion me. W-why?"

Mama put her arms around Jody Ann and hugged her. Mama always smelled like flowers.

"Well, I don't know about Rachel's mama, but I prayed a long time for a little girl. It didn't matter what the doctor—or anybody else—said. I knew you were a special gift from God."

"L-like a present, you mean?"

Mama smiled. "Exactly. And when God gives you a present, you know it'll be wonderful!"

Jody Ann imagined jumping out of a giant box with a big, red bow on it. She smiled. Being a present from God was a nice thing to think about.

⌒

Jody Ann thought about Mama's words all the next day at Little Treasures. When she dropped a whole stack of diapers on the floor, she whispered, "I am . . . a p-present from God." When she couldn't remember the right words, she said, "It's O-K, Jody Ann. Y-you . . . are a present from God."

Near the end of the day, Jody Ann finally got to help in Rachel's room again. She found Rachel alone in a corner, rocking and hitting her toy against the floor.

Jody Ann squatted down beside her. "Hi, Rachel. 'Member me? It's Jody Ann." Rachel let out a happy squawk.

Jody Ann sat down on the floor and put her arms around the little girl. Together, they began to rock back and forth. Then Jody Ann started to sing. "Lit-tle ones to Him be-long . . . "

When she finished singing, Jody Ann whispered in Rachel's ear.

"We are not retards, Rachel. M-mama says . . . we are presents . . . from God. Did you know that?" She tipped her head to look at Rachel's face. "E-everybody loves presents! And I think your mama must love you . . . a whole bunch!" Rachel made a happy sound and leaned her head against Jody Ann's chest.

"Jody Ann?"

Jody Ann looked up and saw her own mama at the door. She grinned.

"Just l-like my m-mama loves me."

Ten Memories
of Growing Up with Mom

1 *The smell of springtime when I hugged her*

2 *Walking hand in hand to the corner store for a special treat*

3 *Doing jigsaw puzzles and arguing over which of us had to do the sky*

4 *Hearing Mom pound out hymns on our old piano*

5 *Making soap sculptures out of Ivory Flakes and water*

6 Getting sleepy during church and resting my head in Mom's oh-so-comfortable lap

7 Evening prayers and good-night kisses

8 Sneaking under the Christmas tree to try to decipher Mom's secret codes on our untagged packages

9 Finding Mom asleep in her chair, "waiting up" for me to come home from a date

10 The countless times she cheered me on

thank

you...

*for loving me, even in my
most unlovable moments.*

I Will Remember

I don't remember my mother showing me how to say my prayers, or the first time she taught me the words to "Jesus Loves Me"—but I know she did. The prayers and the songs of faith from my childhood are deeply ingrained in my spirit—a legacy handed down to a daughter from a mother who wanted her little girl to know God.

I don't remember, but I can imagine my mother kneeling with me beside my bed, her hands folded around mine. I hear her simple prayer, spoken one short phrase at a time, followed by my hit-and-miss echo: "God . . . Daddy . . . Mommy . . . Brother . . . Amen."

I don't remember, but I can almost hear my mother singing as she ironed Daddy's shirts or swept the kitchen floor. "Jesus loves me, this I know . . . " I imagine playing close by, the words burrowing deep into my soul.

I don't remember my mother planting those early seeds of faith, nor did I witness the private tears and prayers that watered them. But the harvest speaks for itself.

I have knelt beside my own little girls and listened to them pray. The words to "Jesus Loves Me" and a hundred other songs have echoed through the halls of our home and traveled with us in our car.

And someday, when my daughters are grown and they pass along this spiritual inheritance to their own children, I will remember. A mother's love planted the first seed.

Teach your children to choose the

right path, and when they are older,

they will remain upon it.

—Proverbs 22:6 NLT

My dear, sweet mom,

   If a mother's job is to teach her child, you're a huge success! I've learned so much from you, from practical skills to gems of wisdom. But the most important thing you've taught me is how to love—how to make others feel special. It was the easiest lesson I've ever learned, because that's what you did for me. And I'll never forget.

                                        Your appreciative child

Dear heavenly Father,

What a blessing my mother has been to me! I thank You for her life and for the influence she has had on mine. From the beginning, she has helped shape me into the person I am becoming. Help me daily to remember her faithfulness, her love, and the sacrifices she made on my behalf.

Father, I ask that You lavish every great gift on this incredible woman who gave me life. As she has cared for me, care for her. Hold her in Your loving arms as she once cradled me. Give her a heart of peace, Lord, and let her know the irreplaceable role she plays in my life.

Thank You, Father, for the love that binds us to each other—and to You.

Amen